A Potpourri
Of Trivia

A Potpourri Of Trivia

Volume One

J.C. Harding

authorHOUSE®

AuthorHouse™LLC
1663 Liberty Drive
Bloomington, IN 47403
www.authorhouse.com
Phone: 1-800-839-8640

Published by AuthorHouse   09/24/2013

ISBN: 978-1-4918-1779-7 (sc)
ISBN: 978-1-4918-1778-0 (e)

Any people depicted in stock imagery provided by Thinkstock are models, and such images are being used for illustrative purposes only. Certain stock imagery © Thinkstock.

This book is printed on acid-free paper.

Because of the dynamic nature of the Internet, any web addresses or links contained in this book may have changed since publication and may no longer be valid. The views expressed in this work are solely those of the author and do not necessarily reflect the views of the publisher, and the publisher hereby disclaims any responsibility for them.

Dedication

A special dedication to my sisters, Nancy Miller and Georgia "Jody" Mapes for the loving care they gave Stacy for 30 years. Also to Lea Ann Bettis for caring for Stacy in the final two years of her life.

Also to all my family and to all my friends that called to say they had a trivia question for me.

The idea of this book came about a year ago. I spent countless hours at the nursing home with my daughter, Stacy. I read to pass the time. She could not talk or walk due to her injuries. I got the idea to start the book. I have always been an avid reader of any and everything. After my husband passed away and I was recovering from two hip surgeries, I would read five to six paperback books a week. I became interested in Trivia when the first home game was introduced. When I came across an interesting question while reading, I would write it down. I have pursed over five hundred books and magazines of every genre and watch all the educational programs on television. This book was a labor of love since it was composed in long hand. I guess I am one of the only people not owning a computer?

I hope you enjoy this book as much as I did composing it.

"Ciao"

References

Over 500 books of every genre

All types of magazines

Brochures from museums, amusement parks, travel stops and service stations.

Most of all my movie trivia come from my home video collection (200).

The answers to each page of questions are on the reverse of the page with matching numbers. NO CHEATING!

1. Which actor was the original voice of "Charlie the Tuna"?

2. What was the name of the head pig in George Orwells "Animal Farm" film? (1994 Film)

3. Which candy was originally produced for the military?

4. What was Elton John's middle name?

5. Name Woody the Woodpecker's girlfriend?

6. Before becoming an actress, she was a makeup artist for a funeral home.

7. What is the Spanish name for San Francisco Bay's island, "Alcatrus"?

8. What is the approximate fraction of an iceberg appearing above the waterline, regardless of size?

9. In the poem, "Casey at the Bat", what was the final score of the game?

10. In the movie "A Star is Born" starring Barbra Streisand, this song won Best Song Category?

1. Herschel Bernard

2. Napoleon

3. M & M

4. Hercules

5. Winnie

6. Whoopi Goldberg

7. Pelican

8. 1/9th

9. 3-2

10. Evergreen

11. Name of the feisty young lady who does the commercial for Progressive Insurance?

12. What were the total sales on the first day of business of the New York Macy's on October 28, 1858?

13. How many color circles are on the vinyl sheet in the game "Twister"?

14. What size shoe does Olive Oyl wear?

15. What was the top price of a ticket to the first Super Bowl game in 1967?

16. What was the last word of all episodes titles of the TV series "The Man from Uncle"?

17. What is the technical term for a collector of teddy bears?

18. Which president could not read or write until his wife taught him?

19. What baby animal gains 10 pounds an hour?

20. How many marines are in the famous photograph "Raising the Flag on Iwo Jima"? (Feb 23, 1945)

21. Who had a horse name "Pokey"?

11. Flo

12. $11.06

13. 24

14. 14-AAAAAA

15. $12.00

16. Affair

17. Arctophile

18. Andrew Johnson

19. Blue whale

20. Five Marines and 1 Navy corpsman

21. Gumby

22. What was the name of Barbie's Palomino horse?

23. How did Attila the Hun die?

24. Cole Porter was a member of which branch of the military?

25. What junk food is the most popular in U.S. households?

26. Ophidiophobia is the fear of what?

27. Which U.S. citizen was the first billionaire?

28. What year was daylight savings time started?

29. Before becoming a writer, what was the occupation held by Aesop?

30. What is the average lifespan of a termite?

31. What is Donald Duck's middle name?

32. Who was the first host of the game show "The Price is Right"?

33. What body of lakes has the largest supply of fresh water on earth?

34. Which plant gives root beer its fizz?

22. Dallas

23. Choked to death from a nosebleed

24. French Foreign Legion

25. Potato Chips

26. Snakes

27. J.D. Rockefeller

28. 1918

29. Slave

30. 30 years

31. Fontaroy

32. Bill Cullen

33. Great Lakes

34. Yucca

35. What people developed a breed of dog for the table?

36. What gentleman is buried in London with his wife and mistress?

37. Name the only two breed of dog that has a black tongue?

38. Who was named the "King of Glitter Rock"?

39. Which game show host coined the phrase "Back in two and two"?

40. Which is the longest island in the continental U.S.?

41. Who gave King Arthur the sword Excalibur?

42. In the 1938 movie "Bringing up Baby", what was baby?

43. How much money was found in President Lincoln's pocket when was assassinated?

44. What author's real name is Theodore Geisel?

45. Who did President Ford pardon on his last day in office?

35. Aztec

36. Carl Marx

37. Chow, Sharpe

38. David Bowie

39. Chuck Woolery

40. Whidbey Island

41. Lady of the Lake

42. Leopard

43. 5 Confederate Five dollar bill

44. Dr. Seuss

45. Tokyo Rose

46. This drink was first served at the 1904 State Fair.

47. Which movie star's real name is Lislie Hornby?

48. What comedian coined the phrase "If it's bigger than a bread box"?

49. Which actor did the voice of the Grinch in the film "The Grinch who stole X-mas"?

50. Where is the largest airport in the world located?

51. What did John Lennon have in the back seat of his Rolls Royce?

52. In which country was the greyhound dog bred?

53. What does the "K" on canned goods stand for?

54. What is the name of the Oscar award given to animals?

55. Name of the only Destroyer in WWII to sink without the loss of a single man?

56. What was the name of the dead man used to dupe Hitler in the maneuver called "Operation Mincemeat"?

46. Iced Tea

47. Twiggy

48. Steve Allen

49. Boris Karloff

50. Saudi Arabia

51. Double Bed

52. Egypt

53. Kosher

54. Patsy

55. USS William D Portor

56. Glyndwr Micheal

57. In WWII, which boat builder stole raw material from an oil refinery in Texas to build landing barges?

58. Name of the guerrilla ally whose life was saved by OSS Deer Team (1945) later to become "America's Public Enemy Number One"?

59. What did security guard Frank Welles find in the basement of the "Offices of Democratic National Committee" that toppled President Nixon on June 17, 1972.

60. Why did the pilgrims remain at Plymouth Rock instead of sailing on to Virginia?

61. Which baseball player swatted the longest homerun ever hit in Yankee Stadium (580 feet longer than anyone else)?

62. What movie star said he based his portrayal of a western lawman on his conversations with Wyatt Earp?

63. This famous lawman died at his desk, at the New York Telegram offices (with his boots on)?

64. The birth of which legendary city do we have to thank Attila the Hun for?

57. Andrew Jackson Higgins

58. Hochi Minh (1945)

59. Masking tape on basement door lock

60. They ran out of beer

61. Josh Gibson

62. John Wayne

63. Bat Materson

64. Venice, Italy

65. Who was the first person to declare smoking bad for the lungs?

66. Which pastry was copied from the enemies flag and first baked in 1683

67. Lloyds of London became famous for insuring which film star's legs for one million dollars?

68. To whom is the invention of Rag paper credited to?

69. Who is credited for inspiring inventors to make paper out of wood pulp?

70. Who composed the hymn "Amazing Grace"?

71. At whose funeral was all the burial attendants murdered so they could not reveal his burial location?

72. Which herb was so esteemed by the Native Indians, they would throw it in the fire as a sacrifice to the gods?

73. Who was the most successful pirate of all times?

74. What famous actor saved President Lincoln's son from being run over by a train?

65. King James I (1605)

66. Croissant (1683)

67. Betty Grable

68. Ts Ai Lun (Eunich)

69. Rene Antoine Reaumur

70. Slave trader John Newman

71. Attila the Hun

72. Uppowoc (Tobacco in English)

73. Cheng I Sao (wife of Pirate Cheng Yih) 1807

74. Edwin Booth (John Wilkes Booth's brother)

75. On the same night of the Chicago fire (Oct. 8, 1871), what town in Wisconsin had one of the deadliest fires in history?

76. How much did the largest diamond ever found weigh (1905)?

77. Which Disney character owns three cubic acres of money?

78. What desert animal never drinks water?

79. Name of the highest nautical lake in the world.

80. What is the name of Olive Oyl's brother?

81. In what NYC night club did the twist fad start?

82. Name of the rare metal that Wonder Woman's bracelets are made.

83. Which state did the first female senator represent?

84. Which cartoonist hosted the 50's TV game show "Anyone can Win"?

85. On the TV's "Mary Hartman" series, what were the names of Loretta Hoger's two goldfish?

75. Pebtigo, Wisconsin (1871)

76. 3106 carats

77. Uncle Scrooge

78. Addax Antelope

79. Lake Titicaca

80. Castor Oyl

81. Peppermint Lounge

82. Feminum

83. Arkansas (Hattie Carway)

84. Al Capp

85. Conway and Twiddy

86. Pat Patton is the side kick of this comic strips character.

87. Who coined the phrase "The Jazz Age"?

88. Whose figure was used as a model for Tinker Bell?

89. What did Telley Savalas keep in his mouth on the TV series "Kojak"?

90. How many crew members were on the original Star Trek spaceship "Enterprise NCC-1701"?

91. What snack food was introduced to the colonist by the Native Indians?

92. Which comedian played the postman on radio's "The Fanny Brice Show"?

93. What school did the girls in the film "The Group" attend?

94. What former budding male child star was in the TV series "The People's Choice" in 1955?

95. What is the name of Count Dracula's twenty acre residence near London?

86. Dick Tracy

87. F. Scott Fitzgerald

88. Marilyn Monroe

89. Tootsie Roll Pop

90. 430

91. Popcorn

92. Danny Thomas

93. Vasser

94. Jackie Cooper

95. Colfax Abbey

96. This musician was named "America's Ambassador of Goodwill" to the world.

97. On what holiday does a gigantic tidal wave occur in the film "The Poseidon Adventure"?

98. What soap opera was interrupted by Walter Cronkite to announce the shooting of John F Kennedy?

99. Jerry Mahoney was the dummy of which ventriloquist?

100. This actor was nicknamed "The Vagabond Lover"

101. What profession did Perry Como pursue before becoming a singer?

102. What American president was sworn in by his father?

103. According to legend, who was the only man to glimpse Lady Godiva's notorious ride?

104. He literally stole the film "Mr. Roberts" from Henry Fonda and James Cagney.

105. How many rooms are in the White House?

106. What make of car did TV's Laverne & Shirley" drive?

96. Louis Armstrong

97. New Year's Eve

98. "As the World Turns"

99. Paul Winchell

100. Rudy Valli

101. Barbering

102. John Calvin Coolidge

103. A tailor named Tom (peeping)

104. Jack Lemmon

105. 32

106. Hudson convertible

107. Dodge City was base camp in the Vietcong Territory in which 1968 movie?

108. What was the name of Elvis Presley's first movie?

109. What was Jim Anderson's profession on the TV series "Father Knows Best"?

110. Name of the step that Chuck Berry danced on stage?

111. What make of plane did the Red Barron fly?

112. Name of the dish consisting of peas, carrots and chicken in cream sauce, created by Thomas Jefferson.

113. In the music world, who was known as the "Great Mister B"?

114. Which special flavor of ice cream did Baskin-Robins create for the Beatles first American tour?

115. What type of wood was used to build Noah's ark?

116. Name of the bar that TV's "Peter Gunn" used as a hangout.

117. What pop artist designed the original package for Campbell's' dry soup mix?

107. "Green Beret"

108. "Love Me Tender"

109. Insurance salesman

110. Duck Walk

111. A Fokker Triplane

112. Chicken ala King

113. Billy Eckstine

114. Beatle Nut

115. Gopher wood

116. Mothers

117. Andy Warhol

118. The first piano was reportedly built in which Italian city?

119. Who played the simple-minded giant in the film "Of Mice and Men"?

120. Which actor from TV's "This Gun for Hire" stood on a box for many of his love scenes?

121. In what musical key do most American automobiles horns beep?

122. In what country was sign language developed?

123. What was Gayety's medicated paper?

124. Which cartoon characters did Gene Kelly dance with in the film "Anchors Aweigh"?

125. In a military academy graduation address, which U.S. Senator said "War is hell"?

126. Who was the first president to ride on a train?

127. In what country was naval hero John Paul Jones born?

118. Florence (1720)

119. Lon Chaney

120. Alan Ladd

121. The key of 'F'

122. Germany

123. First U.S. manufactured toilet paper

124. Jerry the Mouse

125. William Tecumsch Sherman

126. Andrew Jackson

127. Scotland

128. Composer pop-star Randy Newman received hate mail for composing what song?

129. Which crooner received the first singing telegram in 1933?

130. Who starred as a "good-luck charm" on each season opening of the "Carol Burnett Show"?

131. What kind of animal was featured in the film "Once Upon a Time" starring Cary Grant?

132. The first televised U.S. presidential speech was given by what president?

133. The croissant was created by Europeans to celebrate whose defeat?

134. Which western actors voice was used for six of the "Frances the Talking Mule" films?

135. Which comedienne was the first woman to receive the "Friar's Club" life achievement award?

136. Nancy Hanks was the mother to which American president?

137. In what film did Jerry Lewis play seven different parts?

128. "Short People"

129. Rudy Valli

130. Jim Nabors

131. Caterpillar

132. Harry Truman

133. The Turks

134. Chill Wills

135. Lucille Ball

136. Abe Lincoln

137. "Family Jewels"

138. In 1965, after the shipwreck of the RHU Lyn, how many hours did Bonnie Rhydwen swim before reaching land?

139. In CB jargon, what is a trucker carrying if he has a "load of post holes"?

140. Name of the computer used in the film "Aliens" starring Sigourney Weaver?

141. What gauge is the U.S standard railroad tie?

142. When truckers meet the "White Knight", what are the facing?

143. In what year was the U.S. Supreme Court organized?

144. Who was the first animal to be admitted to the Animal Hall of Fame in 1969?

145. What profession did James Mason pursue before he became an actor?

146. In 1071, Jacqueline Cochran was the first woman to be elected to which hall of fame?

147. In 1975, Boys who join this organization are called 'Blue Jays' and 'Thunderbirds'.

138. 16 Hours

139. Nothing

140. Mother

141. 4" x 8 1/2"

142. State patrol

143. 1789

144. Lassie

145. Architect

146. Aviation

147. Camp Fire Boys and Girls, later to be camp fire USA.

148. Which western film star carried a whip as his trademark?

149. "Zahra" means brilliant and originates from which language?

150. What is the original meaning for the word museum?

151. Name of the comic who played the postman on radio's "The Fanny Brice" show?

152. What was disc jockey Murray the K's last name?

153. Give the acronym for the mutual security treaty involving Australia, New Zealand and the U.S.?

154. Which famous actor did the voice of Cleo the Goldfish in the 1940 film "Pinocchio"?

155. What cigarette brand sponsored radio's "Your Hit Parade"?

156. Which female personality hosted the radio show "Blind Date" in 1945?

157. The Star Trek Enterprise was on a mission for how many years?

148. Lash Larue

149. Arabic

150. Temple of the Muses

151. Danny Thomas

152. Kaufman

153. Anzus

154. Mel Blanc

155. Lucky Strike

156. Arlene Francis

157. Five years

158. In bullfighting, which horseman tires the bull before the matador enters the ring?

159. How many crew members were on the original Enterprise of TV's "Star Trek" that first aired on TV on September 8, 1966?

160. Name of the U.S. Naval vessel seized by the Koreans in 1968?

161. Name of the mascot of the 1984 summer Olympic Games.

162. It is the southernmost city in the contiguous 48 States.

163. Name of the screen process introduced by Mike Todd and first used in the film "Oklahoma".

164. Which airport has two churches and a synagogue on it's grounds?

165. What breed of dog was first to be registered in the U.S.?

166. Name of the gambling yacht on the TV series "Mr. Lucky".

167. In the 1950's, who closed down the restaurants and theaters of American on Tuesday nights at 8 pm?

158. Picador

159. 450

160. USS Pueblo

161. Sam the Eagle

162. Key West, Florida

163. Todd-AO

164. Kennedy

165. English Settler (1878)

166. Fortuna

167. Milton Berle

168. "The Singing Brakeman" is the nickname of which country singer?

169. U.S. gold is stored in Fort Knox, where is the silver stored?

170. What brand of ice cream was in a "Dixie Cup"?

171. Mary Hartline was leader of the band on which TV series?

172. In what film did a whole town attempt to give up smoking in thirty days?

173. He was leader of a Latin band and also a talented caricaturist.

174. What politician's life was the film "All the Kings Men" based on?

175. Afloat what color are odd number buoys?

176. What was Harry Bliss' automotive claim to fame?

177. Who succeeded "Bloody Mary" to the throne of England?

178. Which American anthem was originally titled "The Defense of Fort McHenry"?

168. Jimmie Rodgers

169. West Point

170. Meadow Gold

171. Super Circus

172. Cold Turkey

173. Xavier Cugat

174. Huey Long

175. Black

176. First car accident victim (1899)

177. Elizabeth I

178. "Star Spangled Banner"

179. Name of the basset hound on the TV series "The People's Choice".

180. On which knee does the right arm of Roden's famous statue "The Thinker" rest?

181. The comic strip Buck Rogers dates back to what year?

182. Name of the clown played by James Stewart in the film "The Greatest Show on Earth".

183. Chic Young created what comic strip?

184. Lauren Chapin played "baby" on which TV family sitcom?

185. Where are Panama hats made?

186. Who founded the University of Virginia?

187. In the fourteenth century what was extracted from the head of the toad and used to treat poisoning?

188. In ancient times, what gem was used to stop nosebleeds?

189. What does the pyrometer measure?

179. Cleo

180. Left

181. 1929

182. Buttons

183. Blondie

184. "Father Knows Best"

185. Ecuador

186. Thomas Jefferson

187. Bufotenine

188. Heliotrope

189. The density of gems

190. In 1866, name the young man who discovered the first diamond in South Africa?

191. What product was the sponsor of the original TV show "What's My Line"?

192. Name of the Navy cruiser launched by author Margaret Mitchell.

193. The first census in 1790 recorded the U.S. population at about how many million?

194. What movie was being shown aboard Columbia Airline flight 409 in the film "Airport 75"?

195. What is the name of the fans that followed Arnold Palmer around the golf course during competition?

196. Lily Tomlin's "Edith Ann" has a dog name what?

197. Which WWII general competed in the 1912 Olympic pentathlon?

198. In the Northern Hemisphere, water drains in which direction?

199. The Patagonian steppes dominate the southern part of what country?

200. Who were the background singers of "Mrs. Robinson" and "The Sound of Silence" in the film "The Graduate"?

190. Erasmus Jacob's

191. Geritol

192. Atlanta (1941)

193. Four million

194. America Graffiti

195. Arnie's Army

196. Buster

197. George Patton

198. Counter clockwise

199. Argentina

200. Simon & Garfunkel

201. Gene Autry was the first star in what "type" of western movie?

202. Which was the first successful mass-produced automobile?

203. What Ottawa Chief attempted to drive the British out of North America?

204. What was Pittsburg's name as a French settlement?

205. In what country was Charlie Chan born?

206. A pop fly that falls between the infielder and outfielder is called what?

207. What male animal offers a female a pebble, if she accepts; they build a nest of stones together?

208. Who created the comic strip "Terry and the Pirates"?

209. Name of the hometown of Charlie Weaver the character played by Cliff Arguette?

210. What famous event happened at the site of Coventry County?

211. Name of the high school featured in TV's series "Room 222"?

201. Musical

202. Model "N" Ford

203. Pontiac (Chief)

204. Fort Duquesne

205. England

206. Texas Leaguer

207. The Adelie Penguin

208. Milton Cantiff

209. Mt. Idy

210. Lady Godiva's Ride

211. Walt Whitman

212. What was the number of the apartment where the "Jeffersons" lived?

213. What family provided the fire works for President Reagan's inauguration?

214. What local Philadelphia musical TV show made it's network debut in 1957?

215. Who was the boyfriend of Flip Wilson's character "Geraldine"?

216. What was the military religious order of the Middle Ages at the time of the Crusaders called?

217. In what South American country do women wear bowler type hats?

218. In what year was the N.Y. World Trade Center officially opened?

219. What was the name of the 60's TV comedy series starring Paula Prentiss and Richard Benjamin?

220. James Naismith was the inventor of what popular sport?

221. Name of the Island where King Kong was discovered.

212. 120

213. Grucci

214. "American Bandstand"

215. 'Killer'

216. The Knights Templar

217. Bolivia

218. 1972

219. "He & She"

220. Basketball (1891)

221. Skull Island

222. What famous comedienne was born Leslie Townes?

223. Leonard Graves narrated twenty-six episodes of what WWII documentary TV series?

224. What word did journalist Herb Caen coin to describe off-beat artist and philosophers?

225. What detective was never portrayed on film by a member of his race?

226. What is the sacred name of Siddhartha Gautama?

227. What state has the largest number of licensed drivers?

228. Name of the only marsupial that lives in the wilds of Australia.

229. What delicacy imported from France and Italy is now being grown in Texas?

230. Dudley Moore played the role of George Webber in this scintillating movie?

231. What gnomish gnarled tree is older than the redwoods and the sequoias?

222. Bob Hope

223. Victory at Sea

224. Beatniks

225. Charlie Chan

226. Buddha

227. California

228. Possum

229. Black Truffles

230. "Ten"

231. Bristlecone pine

232. What male singing legend hosted the "Bulova Watch Time" musical variety show on radio in 1950?

233. What country do the Gurkhas call home?

234. What household "necessity" did Cecil H. Booth invent in 1905?

235. Name of the river that flows near the area of 'Custer's last stand'?

236. What actress married convicted murderer Cotton Adamson White while he was still in prison?

237. In 1937, who narrated "You are There", TV's dramatic recreation of historical events?

238. In what year did Wyoming elect the first U.S. woman governor?

239. "Roll Over Beethoven" was re-recorded by what band in 1964?

240. On September 21, 1802, Benedict Arnold negotiated with what British spy for the betrayal of West Point?

241. What type of colony was the first settlement in Sydney, Australia in 1788?

232. Frank Sinatra

233. Nepal

234. Vacuum cleaners

235. Little Big Horn

236. Sue Lyons

237. Walter Cronkite

238. 1925

239. The Beatles

240. John André, British Mayor

241. Penal Colony

242. What artist is considered the "Queen of Rhythm and Blues"?

243. What fee did Burt Reynolds receive for his "Cosmopolitan" nude centerfold?

244. The black district in the musical "Porgy and Bess" was called what?

245. What state was the first to legalize the lottery?

246. What type of contest was featured in the movie "They Shoot Horse, Don't They?"

247. What TV program originated the concept of "Rate a Record"?

248. What comedienne closed his TV Show with "Goodnight, Mrs. Calabash, where ever you are"?

249. What type of animal is the "merganser"?

250. What is the correct title of the song often referred to by it's first line?

251. What insect, native to Italy, can throw its voice like a Ventriloquist.

242. Lauren Baker

243. None

244. Catfish Row

245. New Hampshire

246. Marathon Dancing

247. "American Bandstand"

248. Jimmie Durante

249. Duck

250. "Music Music Music"

251. Cricket

252. What Broadway show was based on "Romeo and Juliet"?

253. What is the valuable fur of the coypu called?

254. He played the role of the Sergeant Chip Saunders in the TV series "Combat".

255. Which newspaper does Oscar Madison work for in the TV series "Odd Couple"?

256. Miyoshi Umike played the role of Mrs. Livingston, Tom and Eddie Corbett's housekeeper on what TV series?

257. What is the nautical slang for throwing something overboard?

258. What is the popular name for the animals also known as cullauenes and bangarroos?

259. What box number did Lincoln occupy the night of his assignation?

260. Name of the rich, temperate plains of East Central Argentina.

261. The horn of the rhinoceros is composed of what?

252. "West Side Story"

253. Nutria

254. Vic Marrows

255. The New York Herald

256. "The Courtship of Eddie's Father"

257. Deep six

258. Koalas

259. Seven

260. The Pampas

261. Hair-fused together

262. Which flower did the ancient Greeks dedicate to the god's of sleep, dream and death?

263. What year was the first basketball game broadcast on radio?

264. In what battle did Oliver Hazard Perry defeat the British?

265. Humphrey Bogart played the role of this boat captain in the film "The African Queen"?

266. Anaheim, Azusa and Cucamonga were train stops on whose radio show?

267. In this film, Janet Gaynor's last words were "Hello, my name is Mrs. Norman Maine"?

268. Who performed the famous beach scene in the film "From Here to Eternity"?

269. Who performed the role of a gangster named "Noodles" in the film "Once Upon A Time In America"?

270. Who composed the theme song for the "Tonight Show"?

271. How many years did it take to build the Sears Tower?

262. Poppy

263. 1921, KDKA Pittsburg

264. Battle of Lake Erie

265. Charlie Alnut

266. Jack Benny

267. The original "A Star Is Born"

268. Burt Lancaster and Donna Reed

269. Robert DeNiro

270. Paul Anka

271. Four

272. According to legend, King Arthur was taken to this island paradise after his death?

273. What is the second highest mountain range in the world?

274. Rosecliff, a Newport mansion, was designed by which famous architect?

275. Richard Basehart and David Hedison were featured in what "wet" TV series?

276. From 1952 to 1966, What radio and TV comedy series was based on the real life situations of a real American family?

277. "Playboy" magazine's first issue was published in what year?

278. Name of the first Norwegian to reach the South Pole in December of 1911?

279. What marsh plant did American Indians use as food for flour and also for burns?

280. What was the first name of movie land's "Citizen Kane"?

281. What is the last movement of a musical composition called?

272. Avalon

273. Andes

274. Sandford White

275. "Voyage to the Bottom of the Sea"

276. "The Adventures of Ozzie and Harriet"

277. 1953

278. Roald Amundsen

279. Cattails

280. Charles

281. The finale

282. This fossil's resin is used in making beads and ornaments.

283. What once was man's main means of defense and livelihood now has evolved into this sport?

284. Which was the first alphabet school letter to be given for a collegiate sport?

285. What color is a chameleon at night?

286. He gives out "The Golden Fleece Awards" for wasteful spending by the government.

287. What is the name of Howdy Doody's sister?

288. German brides carry this herb for good luck.

289. Who composed the best-selling theme song on TV's "Peter Gunn"?

290. The skin consists of how many million nerve endings that detect pain?

291. Name of the longest running radio drama (1932-1959)?

292. What is the nearest continent to Antarctica?

282. Amber

283. Archery

284. "C"

285. Blue

286. William Proxmire

287. Heidi Doody

288. Dill

289. Henry Mancini

290. Four

291. "One Man's Family"

292. South America

293. What was the name of Cornelius Vanderbilt's 185 foot yacht?

294. The shortest route across the English Channel is between Dover and this French City?

295. How many languages are used for simultaneous interpretation at the U.N.?

296. Tiny Tim & Miss Vickey exchanged marriage vows on this TV talk show?

297. "God Enriches" is the motto of this southwestern state?

298. Who sang lead vocals for "Big Brother and the Holding Company"?

299. From 1972 to 1974, Helen Hayes and Mildred Natwick co-starred in this mystery TV series?

300. What city has been the site of the most presidential nominations?

301. In 1938, What actor starred only in the first Dr. Kildair's films?

293. The Atlantic

294. Calis

295. Six (Arabic, Spanish, French, Chinese, English and Russian)

296. "The Tonight Show"

297. Arizona

298. Janis Joplin

299. Snoop Sisters

300. Chicago

301. Joel McCrea

302. What member of the Cartwright family has a horse name "Cochise" in the TV series "Bonanza"?

303. Name of the highest mountains in New York.

304. President Franklin D. Roosevelt nominated how many approved Supreme Court Justices?

305. Who was the original star of Broadway's "Mr. Wonderful"?

306. Who was the first black world heavyweight champion?

307. She was the mother of King Solomon.

308. What was the photographer's nickname in the "Lou Grant" TV series?

309. In what year did the first person collect Social Security?

310. Name the state tree of Alaska.

311. George Maharis portrayed "Buz Murdock" in this TV series.

312. Pluto is the pet dog to this cartoon character.

313. What grade did Gerald Ford reach as a Boy Scout?

302. Little Joe

303. Mt. Marcy

304. Nine

305. Sammy Davis, Jr.

306. Jack Johnson

307. Bathsheba

308. Animal

309. 1940

310. The Sitka tree

311. Route 66

312. Mickey Mouse

313. Eagle Scout

314. Name the two actors who were with Natalie Wood at the time of her death.

315. Who was the "Sock-It-To-Me Girl" on Rowan and Martin's "Laugh-In"?

316. Who played "Mr. Lucky" in the 1943 movie by the same name?

317. How many days after the U.S. declared war on Japan did Germany declare war on the U.S.?

318. This American was the first to force a British Naval squadron to surrender.

319. Name of the largest and most powerful nuclear submarine of the Trident class.

320. Who was Gene Kelly's dancing partner in the film "American in Paris"?

321. In what Ohio city was John Wilkes Booth's last performance before he assassinated President Lincoln?

322. What is the second largest land mammal?

323. "Out of the Fog, Out of the Night" was the program opening for this radio police series?

314. Robert Wagner and Christopher Walden

315. Judy Carnes

316. Cary Grant

317. Three

318. Oliver Hazard Perry

319. USS Ohio

320. Lesle Caron

321. Cleveland

322. Hippopotamus

323. "Adventures of Bulldog Drummond"

324. In what comic strip do husband and wife wear horned helmets?

325. What actor did M.G.M dub "The Man with the Perfect Face"?

326. In 1848, he died with the distinction of having been the richest man.

327. Who made the hit recording of "Under the Boardwalk"?

328. This comedienne was married to Edgar Rosenberg?

329. What was the nickname of the whale that wandered up California's Sacramento River?

330. He won the Oscar for portraying George M. Cohen in the film "Yankee Doodle Dandy.

331. The five stars of the constellation Cassiopeia form this letter of the alphabet.

332. In what U.S. city was the first acknowledged skyscraper built?

333. What are Florida's baseball spring training games called?

334. Which American patriot was on French Diplomatic duty and unable to help form the U.S. Constitution?

335. Which actor singer is particularly associated with the song "Donkey Serenade"?

324. Hagar the Horrible

325. Robert Taylor

326. John Jacob Astor

327. The Drifters

328. Joan Rivers

329. Humphrey

330. James Cagney

331. W

332. Chicago

333. Grapefruit League

334. Thomas Jefferson

335. Allen Jones

336. In what U.S. state was the first football stadium built?

337. The process of evolution by survival of the fittest is the called what?

338. What occupation did Red Skeleton's father pursue?

339. "Wasn't it pleasant o' brother mine, In those days of lost sunshine", are the first two lines of this famous poem?

340. When asked the direct question as to his age, this poet replied, "I am this side of forty"?

341. This Canadian officer composed the poem "In Flanders Fields"?

342. What Army rank did Joyce Kilmer hold when he composed the poem "Trees"?

343. In bygone times, Ingersoll was noted for making what dollar item?

344. Who played the role of Joe on TV's "The Hardy Boys"?

345. When Babe Ruth hit his homer in 1927, whose single season record did he break?

346. What phrase never said by Cary Grant helped make him famous?

347. In what month is National Hot Dog Day celebrated?

336. Massachusetts (Harvard)

337. Natural Selectio

338. Circus Clown

339. "Out to Old Aunt Mary's"

340. James Whitcomb Riley

341. Lt. Col. John McCrae

342. Sergeant

343. Pocket watch

344. Shawn Cassidy

345. His own (59 in 1921)

346. Judy, Judy, Judy

347. July

348. What country contains ¼ of the world's trees?

349. Who played the role of Nels in the original Broadway production of "I Remember Mama"?

350. Reportedly, the most common mental health problem is what?

351. In South Africa what is the meaning of "steop"?

352. In what city was the first "Hard Rock Café"?

353. In cooking, how many drops make a dash?

354. Give the literal African meaning of the word aardvark.

355. What year did Reggie Jackson hit his 500th home run?

356. In what city is the world's largest bell located?

357. What was the first song to win an Oscar?

358. Which president-elect was asked to resign from the Army because of heavy drinking?

359. Where are the Funeral Mountains located?

360. Who portrayed "Count Dracula" in the film "Love at First Bite"?

361. What the last name of TV's "Maude"?

362. The movie "Never Say Never Again" marked the return of this actor to what role?

348. Siberia

349. Marlon Brando

350. fear

351. Veranda in front of the house

352. London

353. six

354. Earth Pig

355. 1984

356. Moscow, Russia

357. The Continental

358. Ulysses S. Grant

359. east of Death Valley

360. George Hamilton

361. Findley

362. Sean Connery as James Bond

363. What man designed the first Ferris Wheel for Chicago's 1893 World's Fair?

364. Alice Lon of TV's "The Lawrence Welk Show" was called this name.

365. In the nursery rhyme, what does Little Tommy Tucker sing for?

366. General Mathew Ridgeway replaced which general as head of the Allied Forces in Korea?

367. Which two actors hold the record for most Oscar nominations with no wins?

368. The crusaders introduced what household product to Europe in the Middle Ages?

369. Which movie did Lee Marvin play the role of Cowboy "Kid" Shelleen?

370. Who composed the musical score for the Academy Award movie "Rocky?

371. How many times did the Pony Express riders fail to get the mail through?

372. What was the name of psychologist Bob Hartley's wife of the TV series "The Bob Newhart Show"?

373. England and which other country competed in the first international polo game?

374. Which language contains the most words?

363. George Ferris

364. Champagne Lady

365. His supper

366. Douglas McArthur

367. Richard Burton & Peter O'Toole

368. Sugar

369. Cat Ballou

370. Bill Conti

371. once in 19 months

372. Emily

373. United States

374. English

375. What color blood do most insects have?

376. What do all of the collies who played "Lassie" have in common?

377. Ensign Pavel Chekov was a character on which TV series?

378. From what opera does the music to "Here Comes the Bride" originate?

379. What was the main U.S. Aircraft carrier that brought Doolittle's Raiders to their Tokyo bombing mission?

380. Which cocktail is named for a Scottish outlaw?

381. During the Civil War which side had the most casualties, the Union or the Confederate?

382. Who was the first president to have a desk phone?

383. Which is the largest water fowl in the world?

384. Who played Scarlett O'Hara's father in the film "Gone with the Wind"?

385. What country had the world's largest pyramids?

386. What country was sex therapist Dr. Ruth born?

387. Kate Jackson played the role of a nurse on TVs "The Rookies" before becoming a detective on this TV show.

388. Thomas Howard was the alias of this famous outlaw.

375. mostly colorless

376. They are all males.

377. "Star Trek"

378. "Lohengrin"

379. USS Hornet

380. Rob Roy

381. The Union

382. Herbert Hoover

383. Trumpeter Swan

384. Thomas Mitchell

385. Mexico

386. Germany

387. "Charlie's Angels"

388. Jessie James

389. Lana Turner was supposedly discovered while sipping a soda at this drug store?

390. Master spy Rudolf Abel was traded to the Russians in exchange for which military pilot?

391. Who invented the stock ticker for the Stock Exchange?

392. How many acres encompass the San Francisco Golden Gate Park?

393. How old was Pablo Picasso when his daughter Paloma was born?

394. What did the mermaid in the film "Splash" choose for a name?

395. How old was Mary Lou Retton when she began acrobatics and ballet?

396. What Jack played the role of Morris Buttermaker on TV's "The Bad News Bears?

397. The "Cub Room" was located in which noted N.Y. night club?

398. What symbol appears on the Pope's ring?

399. How old was Shangri La's High Lama in the film "Lost Horizon"?

400. The eagle on the face of the Great Seal of the U.S. holds how many arrows in his talons?

389. The Top Hat Café

390. Francis Gary Powers

391. Thomas Edison

392. One thousand acres

393. 67

394. Madison

395. four years old

396. Jack Warden

397. Stork Club

398. a fish

399. 250 years old

400. thirteen

401. Yellowstone National Park's "Old Faithful" spouts water as high as seven, ten or a twelve story building?

402. Which John was the moderator on TV's "What's My Line"?

403. What do the initials 'M.G.' on the famous British automobile stand for?

404. What swimming stroke did Gertrude Ederle use to cross the English Channel in 1926?

405. What country was the locale for the film "Romancing the Stone"?

406. In terms of chemical compositions what substance does human blood most resemble?

407. Who was the first black man pictured on the U.S. postage-stamp?

408. Who was the girlfriend of Hollywood's Andy Hardy?

409. How many judges are needed for the game Jai-Alai?

410. Which Swede was the screenwriter and director of "Wild Strawberries"?

411. Which presidential wife sponsored the planting of Washington D.C.'s Japanese cherry trees?

412. "Mr. French" was an English gentleman's gentleman on what TV sitcom (1966-1971)?

401. seven

402. John Charles Daly

403. Morris Garage

404. The crawl

405. Colombia

406. Sea water

407. Booker T. Washington

408. Polly Benidict

409. Three

410. Ingmar Bergman

411. William H. Taft (Helen)

412. "Family Affair"

413. How do over 3000 varieties of tea get their name?

414. Flo is the wife of what bulbous nosed comic-strip character?

415. "Dexter Franklin" was the boyfriend to this 1943 radio lady.

416. What two parts of the body contain more sweat glands that any other part?

417. On what 1970's TV drama series did Brother Willie marry a terminally ill girl?

418. Which soft drink celebrated it's 99th birthday in 1985?

419. What singer recorded "To all the Girls I've Loved Before" with Willie Nelson?

420. What kind of wood are most bowling pins made of?

421. In which African country did Jane Goodall do her studies on chimpanzees?

422. Burt Reynolds played the role of Ben Froger on this TV adventure series from 1959 to 1961.

423. What was the largest construction project ever undertaken by man?

424. For which "nosey" role did Jose' Ferrer play to win an Oscar in 1950?

425. Outside of which hotel did the attempted assignation of President Reagan occur on March 30, 1981?

413. from the districts that they are grown in

414. Andy Capp

415. Corless Archer's

416. palm of hand and sole of feet

417. family

418. Coca-Cola

419. Julio Inglesias

420. Maple

421. Tanganyika

422. "River Boat"

423. The Great Wall of China

424. Cyrano de Bergerac

425. Washington Hilton Hotel

426. Which rock group had a hit song "At the Hop"?

427. How many dogs did England's Queen Victoria (1837-1901) own?

428. What actor on TV's "Family" played the role of a F.B.I. Agent in Hollywood's "Dog Day Afternoon"?

429. Name four U.S. capitals that have the first same letter as the name of their state.

430. "Bewitched, Bothered and Bewildered" was first heard in what Broadway musical?

431. Name the father of the Old Testament figure Ham.

432. Which group robbed the San Francisco Hibernia Bank in 1974?

433. What British film was based on the true story of a Jewish Cambridge student and a Scottish missionary?

434. What rock star's dad was a drill instructor in the British Army?

435. What Indian tribe was the most populous in the U.S.?

436. What game has had the most books and articles written about it?

437. Ray Bradbury wrote "Fahrenheit 451" in how many hours?

438. Who helped Gregory Peck discover his real identity in the Hitchcock thriller "Spellbound"?

426. Danny and the Juniors

427. 83

428. James Broderick

429. Dover, Honolulu, Oklahoma City and Indianapolis

430. "Pal Joey"

431. Noah

432. The SLA (including Patty Hearst)

433. "Chariots of Fire"

434. Boy George

435. Navahos

436. Chess

437. twenty hours

438. Ingrid Bergman

439. Who won the Kentucky Derby in 1985?

440. Ingrid Bergman won how many Academy Awards?

441. In what country is the tallest windmill located?

442. What Russian city do many consider the world's biggest fur market?

443. Which is larger a regulation table tennis table or a regulation pool table?

444. What illness did Sister Benidect suffer from in the film "The Bills of St. Mary"?

445. What were Ingrid Bergman's last words in the film "The Bells of St. Mary"?

446. Name of the first president to inhabit the White House.

447. Who is the owner of the comic-strip cat Garfield?

448. What character did John Ratzenberger play on the TV sitcom "Cheers"?

449. What is actor Telly Savalas' first name short for?

450. Giacomo was the first name of which famed Italian opera singer?

451. The world's longest suspension bridge is located in which U.S. city?

439. Spend-a-Buck

440. three

441. Denmark

442. Leningrad

443. pool

444. tuberculosis

445. Just dial "O" for O'Malley

446. John Adams

447. Jon

448. Cliff the postman

449. Aristotle

450. Puccini

451. Verrazano-Narrows Bridge (NY)

452. A Shirley Temple cocktail uses which type of alcohol as it's main ingredient?

453. Broadway's "Barefoot in the Park" was a hit for what director?

454. How many red balls are normally used in a game of snooker?

455. Which desert is three times larger than the Mediterranean Sea?

456. Joe Keipperman was featured in what "brainy" radio program?

457. Which 19th century British Prime Minister was the first Earl of Beaconsfield?

458. Who played the role of Sister Benedict in the film "Belles of St. Mary"?

459. Who was the unofficial First Lady during the administration of widower Thomas Jefferson?

460. The Statue of Liberty holds a torch in one hand, what is in the other hand?

461. Who played the role of housewife Laverne in the "Dirty Linen" segments of her TV show?

462. John Denver was once a singer with this musical trio?

463. What feminist wrote "Sex and the Single Girl"?

452. None

453. Mike Nichols

454. fifteen

455. Sahara Desert

456. "Quiz Kids"

457. Disraeli

458. Ingrid Bergman

459. Dolly Madison

460. open book

461. Cher

462. Chad Mitchell Trio

463. Helen Gurley Brown

464. Which state license plate's motto is "First in Flight"?

465. Whose stage and screen role called for her to answer the phone clad only in a towel?

466. Who was the first woman to win the Nobel Peace Prize?

467. Asked if she intended on changing her playing techniques, which superstar replied "No, I just play my style, 'boring tennis'"?

468. What oddity did Wilber Post own on his TV show?

469. What part of the country do the greatest mountains lay?

470. Which New York City borough hosted American's first tennis games?

471. During a concert, Luciano Pavarotti generally holds what object in his hand?

472. Dustin Hoffman played a female on a soap opera in which movie?

473. Gold coins were last minted in the United States in what year?

474. Which Beatles' single hit record is seven minutes and eleven seconds long?

475. What author wrote the novel "A Many Splendored Thing"?

464. North Carolina

465. Jayne Mansfield

466. Jane Addams (1931)

467. Chris Evert Lloyd

468. talking horse

469. under the sea

470. Staten Island

471. handkerchief

472. "Tootsie"

473. 1933

474. "Hey Jude"

475. Han Suyen

476. Who was the first president to visit a foreign country while in office?

477. Who was the only unseeded tennis player to win the men's singles Wimbledon Championship?

478. Which religious exile founded Rhode Island?

479. Name the first U.S. coin to bear the portrait of an actual person.

480. "Put on a Happy Face" is a song from this Broadway musical.

481. Prince Charles was how much older than Princess Diana?

482. What was the name of the maid on TV's sitcom "The Jeffersons"?

483. How many ways can you make five rolling dice?

484. What musical instrument did 'Little Ricky' play on the TV series "I Love Lucy"?

485. Which Shakespearean character quoted "Out damned spot! Out I say"?

486. Guam is up to 12 miles wide and how many miles long?

487. "Tennessee Waltz" earned a gold record for which musical duo?

476. Theodore Roosevelt (the Panama Canal)

477. Boris Becker (1985)

478. Roger Williams

479. Lincoln penny

480. "Bye, Bye Birdie"

481. twelve years

482. Florence

483. four

484. drums

485. Lady Macbeth

486. thirty miles

487. Les Paul and Mary Ford

488. What was the code name of Hitler's invasion of Russia?

489. Who played the role of Queen Isabella in the TV film "Christopher Columbus"?

490. How many weeks are in the average lifespan of a worker bee?

491. How many midfielders are in each team of the game of lacrosse?

492. What six letter word in the movie "The Moon is Blue" caused trouble with censors?

493. What was "Dennis the Menace's" father's first name?

494. The triangular sail projecting ahead of a ship's foremast is called the what?

495. Which actor portrayed the role of Rowdy Yates in the TV series "Raw Hide"?

496. The Galileo space probe was launched to go to which planet?

497. Which singer had the 1960's hit record "Can't Take my Eyes Off of You"?

498. Name the 1930 Oscar winning anti-war film adapted from Ereck Remarque's novel.

499. What entertainer gave life to the straw hat and the song called "Louise"?

488. "Operation Barbarossa"

489. Faye Dunaway

490. six weeks

491. three

492. virgin

493. Henry

494. Jeb

495. Clint Eastwood

496. Jupiter

497. Frankie Valli

498. "All Quiet on the Western Front"

499. Maurice Chevalier

500. Ellen Corley played the role of Grandma on this family TV series.

501. What brand of ice cream invites you to "enjoy the quiet"?

502. Alan Arkin played the role of a deaf-mute in this film?

503. Where is the palace called the Alhambra located?

504. An astronaut from this country was part of the November 1985 U.S. space shuttle crew?

505. Kam Fong and Zulu played detectives on this 1968 TV series?

506. Who created the character of "Father Knickerbocker" as a symbol for NYC?

507. Name the two oldest colleges in the United States.

508. In what year was the first Kentucky Derby run?

509. "Rosebud" was the last words uttered by this famous actor in the film "Citizen Kane".

510. Who wrote the spy-thriller novel "Mexico Set"?

511. In which N.Y. city was the first Woolworth Dime store opened?

512. Davey Crockett was played by what famous western actor in the film "The Alamo" (1960)?

500. "The Waltons"

501. Frucin Gladje'

502. "The Heart is a Lonely Hunter"

503. Granada, Spain

504. Mexico-Rodolfo Neri

505. "Hawaii Five-O"

506. Washington Irving

507. Harvard and William & Mary

508. 1875

509. Orsen Welles

510. Len Deighton

511. Utica

512. John Wayne

513. King Louis XIV of France was also known by what nickname?

514. Contestants receive "zonks" on this TV game show?

515. A cormorant is a unit of currency, a raisin or a bird?

516. What was the name of the souped-up Dodge Charger on the "Dukes of Hazzard"?

517. On what company label did James Taylor record the song "That's Why I'm Here"?

518. "Tess" was filmed by what tragedy-plagued director?

519. Nermal is the kitten friend of what comic-strip cat?

520. How many children, boys and girls, made up the Von Trapp family?

521. What animal is the bat most closely related to?

522. "Land is the only thing in the world that matters, because it's the only thing that lasts" is a famous quote from what classic movie?

523. Generally, at what age do people begin to shrink?

524. "I Married an Angel" was the singing duo's last film together?

525. Which opera tells the tale of bohemians Mimi and Rudalfo?

513. Sun King

514. "Let's Make a Deal"

515. bird

516. General Lee

517. Columbia

518. Roman Polanski

519. Garfield

520. five girls and two boys

521. cow

522. "Gone With the Wind"

523. Thirty years old

524. Jeannette McDonald and Nelson Eddy

525. "La Boheme"

526. Charle Monche invented what tool?

527. Who was the first U.S. president to ride in a railroad train?

528. Robinson Crusoe spent how many years on his island?

529. According to "cber's" what is the last truck in a convey line called?

530. What is reported to be the favorite sandwich of American's?

531. "Here's looking at you kid" is the famous quote from what classic movie?

532. Name of the deputy sheriff that kept a single bullet in his breast pocket?

533. Which Scottish king is associated with a spider?

534. What disease killed Greta Garbo in the movie "Camelle"?

535. Phillip Michael Thomas of TV's "Miami Vice" has how many children?

536. Who played the role of J.J. on TV's "Good Times"?

537. Which Michael Jackson album preceded his album "Thriller"?

538. What was the Hoover Dam erroneously called from 1935 to 1947?

526. monkey wrench

527. Andrew Jackson

528. 28 years

529. Rubber Duck

530. peanut butter and jelly

531. "Casablanca"

532. Barney Fife

533. Robert Bruce

534. tuberculosis

535. eight

536. Jimmie Walker

537. "Off the Wall"

538. Boulder Dam

539. How many hijackers forced an Egyptian airline to land on Malta in 1985?

540. What was the name of the Douglas' family adopted son on TV's series "My Three Sons"?

541. Which celebrity's son wrote "Going My Own Way"?

542. Linguine is what type of flat food?

543. Recrystallized limestone is known by what common name?

544. Lloyd Haynes played the role of school teacher Pete Dixon on which TV sitcom?

545. What is the most dangerous circus animal act?

546. CD's is a club featured in what 1993 TV Series?

547. The 1993 TV series "Walker, Texas Ranger" takes place in what Texas city?

548. In what year was Pace's picante sauce invented?

549. In 1985, Ed Asner ended his four year term as president of what association?

550. What was the last name of prize fighter/actor "Slapsie Maxie"?

551. In 1985, which charismatic TV correspondent left ABC News after 15 years?

539. five

540. Ernie

541. Bing Crosby

542. pasta

543. marble

544. "Room 222"

545. trained bears

546. "Walker, Texas Ranger"

547. Ft. Worth, Texas

548. 1947

549. Screen Actors' Guild

550. Rosenbloom

551. Geraldo Rivera

552. In 1974, Dustin Hoffman played the role of comedian Lenny Bruce on screen, who played "Bruce" on stage?

553. What was the first name of Lee Harvey Oswald's widow?

554. A mature male 150 pound deer yields about 50, 80 or 100 pounds of venison?

555. The line "sock it to me" is associated with this 1967 TV sitcom?

556. "Kickapoo Joy Juice" is brewed in this comic-strip by Al Capp?

557. Which poet wrote "The Song of Hiawatha"?

558. Goldie Hawn played the role of a giggly dumb blonde on this 1967 TV sitcom?

559. In one night a mole can dig a tunnel how many feet long?

560. Currently, what material is usually used to make arrows?

561. Mae West, Barbara Standwyck and Barbra Streisand were born in what N.Y. city?

562. What African town was named after a United States president?

563. Patty Duke played the role of Anne Sullivan in the TV version of what film?

552. Cliff Gorman

553. Marina

554. 50 pounds

555. "Rowan & Martin's Laugh-In"

556. "Lil Abner"

557. Henry Wadsworth Longfellow

558. "Rowan & Martin's Laugh-In"

559. 300 feet

560. Aluminum

561. Brooklyn, New York

562. Moravia

563. "The Miracle Worker"

564. "Darling, Je Vous Ai'me Beau Coup" was adopted in the mid 1930's for what entertainer's theme song?

565. Who wrote the poem "Sheridan's Ride"?

566. "The winds was a torrent of darkness among the gusty trees" is the first line in this poem by Alfred Noyes?

567. "The Night Before Christmas" was composed by which poet?

568. Kenneth created which first lady's bouffant hair do?

569. In November 1978, Cult leader Jim Jones convinced how many of his followers to kill themselves?

570. Fred Astaire and Gregory Peck appeared together in how many films?

571. Which president quoted "Mankind must put an end to war or war will put an end to mankind"?

572. Who won the special wooden Oscar in 1937?

573. How many times did Charlton Heston play the role of Marc Anthony?

574. Which British rock group compiled fourteen of the top 81 singles of the 1964 charts?

575. Who was Ruby Keeler's most frequent film co-star?

564. Hildegarde

565. Thomas Buchanan Read

566. "The Highwayman"

567. Clement Clarke Moore

568. Jackie Kennedy

569. 913

570. One

571. John F. Kennedy

572. Ventriloquist, Edgar Berger (dummy Charlie McCarthy)

573. Three

574. The Beatles

575. Dick Powell